# 1937-1969
## CLASSIC CHRISTMAS COMIC COVERS

phil-comics

## THE DANDY AND THE BEANO
## CLASSIC CHRISTMAS COMIC COVERS 1937-1969

First published September 2013 by phil-comics

PO Box 2157, Seaford, East Sussex, BN25 9DR
www.phil-comics.com

The Dandy & The Beano are registered trademarks and © D. C. Thomson & Co., Ltd., 2013
Associated characters © D. C. Thomson & Co., Ltd., 2013

Format and concept of this book by Phil Shrimpton
Digital artwork for the design of this book by D. C. Thomson & Co., Ltd

In the production of this book, phil-comics gratefully acknowledges the input and assistance of Martin Lindsay, Gordon Tait and Hilary Mudie, of D. C. Thomson & Co Ltd., for the licensing, digital design and usage of copyright material. My sincere thanks go to Liz Ralph for her endless endurance and support from day one. To Neale Brodie of One Digital, David Jones as an early protagonist of the project and to Irmantas Povilaika for his advice and input. My thanks also go to the Shrimpton and Ralph families for their patience as each new draft for proof reading was thrust under their noses.

All rights reserved. This book is sold subject to the condition that it may not be reproduced, stored in a retrieval system or transmitted in any form or by any means, electronic, mechanical, photocopying, recording or otherwise without the prior consent of the copyright holders.

ISBN: 978-0-9926635-0-6

Printed in England by One Digital, 54 Hollingdean Road, Brighton, East Sussex, BN2 4AA
Bound in England by Skyline Bookbinders, Vincent Lane, Dorking, Surrey, RH4 3HG

10 9 8 7 6 5 4 3 2 1

The Dandy and The Beano comics are two great British institutions which have brought merriment to millions of boys and girls with their anarchic, anti-establishment fun. They began life just before the Second World War and in December 2012 The Dandy turned 75 by going digital after 3,610 print editions were published. The Beano celebrated its 75th birthday in July 2013.

With each comic selling over two million copies per week in the 1950s, there can be very few people in the UK who have not read at least one copy of The Dandy or The Beano as a youngster. Indeed, many readers will have had their own favourite characters - Dennis the Menace, Korky the Cat, The Three Bears and Corporal Clott are some of my own – which have, no doubt, been key factors to the success and longevity of the two comics.

Coupled with a staple of favourite characters, the front covers of the comics were a major attraction – indeed the centrepiece - that were key to securing your weekly subscriptions. The front covers had to be brighter, bolder and more fun than the adjacent title on the news counter. From the very first issues, the front covers of The Dandy and The Beano comics were full colour, packed with laughs and irresistible to the expectant eyes of young boys and girls.

Readers of The Dandy comic laughed at the exploits of its front cover star Korky the Cat. The furry feline was drawn from the very first issue in 1937 through to 1962 by James Crichton, before being succeeded by Charles Grigg.

Big Eggo, an ostrich drawn by Reg Carter, was the cover star of The Beano for ten years, from the first issue. Although popular in the early 1940s, Eggo lost touch with readers and was moved to a small strip inside the comic. Keeping with the theme of animals but with wings becoming paws, in 1948 the great artist Dudley Watkins first illustrated Biffo the Bear as the new cover star of The Beano.

The editors and script writers of The Dandy and The Beano often capitalised on special events throughout the year. Christmas was no exception. Each and every year the Christmas issues were crammed with snow covered title logos, slap-up feasts, Christmas trees, stockings and presents, Christmas puddings, Santa, crackers aplenty and a festive greeting from the editor. Such was the lure of a classic Christmas themed issue that in the early years of 1938, 1939 and 1940, the editors issued more than one Christmas issue per year.

Having first read The Beano comic as a ten year old lad, I've collected pre-1970 copies of The Dandy and The Beano comics and annuals for over twenty years. Throughout that time a stand-out favourite for me has been the Christmas issues. With their fabulous front covers and themed stories throughout, the words 'fun', 'loud', 'bold' and 'vibrant' sprung to mind every time I acquired an elusive issue for my stash.

But it isn't just me who collects them, for the Christmas issues are highly sought after today. As a collector, dealer and online auctioneer of vintage British comics, the level of interest in Christmas issues offered for sale or at auction never ceases to amaze me. It took many years to compile the original comics used in the production of this book - indeed, only a handful of the early issues are known to exist, mainly sequestered in long term private collections.

This book faithfully reprints the stand-alone front covers of every Christmas issue of The Dandy and The Beano comic from 1937 to 1969 inclusive, deemed by many collectors to be the classic years. Given the scarcity of the original issues, I hope this unique compilation of Christmas covers will be a welcome treat to the avid collector, enthusiast, nostalgia seeker and all those fondly remembering their favourite weekly comic treat.

With best wishes,
**Phil Shrimpton**
www.phil-comics.com

September 2013

## KORKY THE CAT

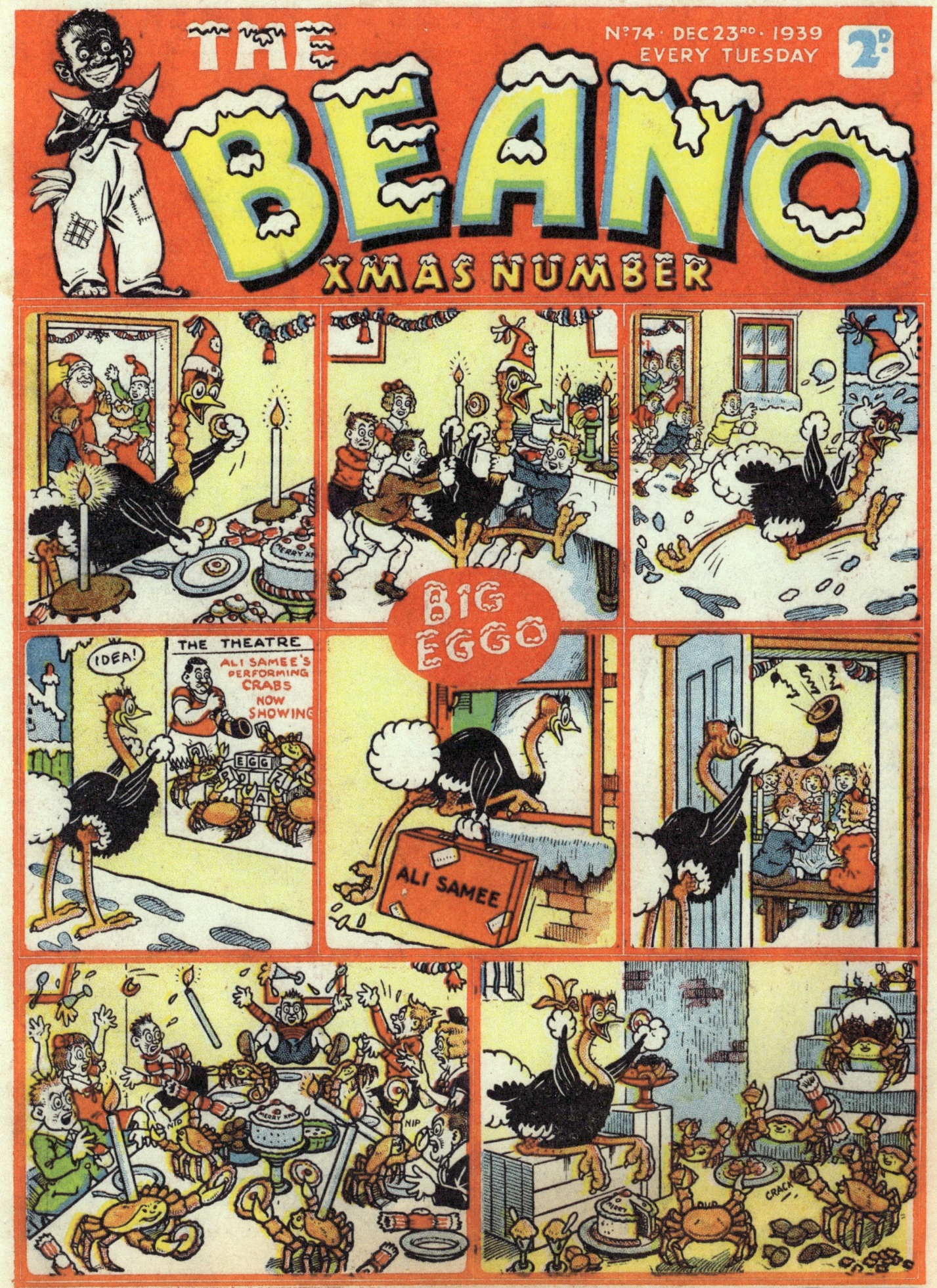

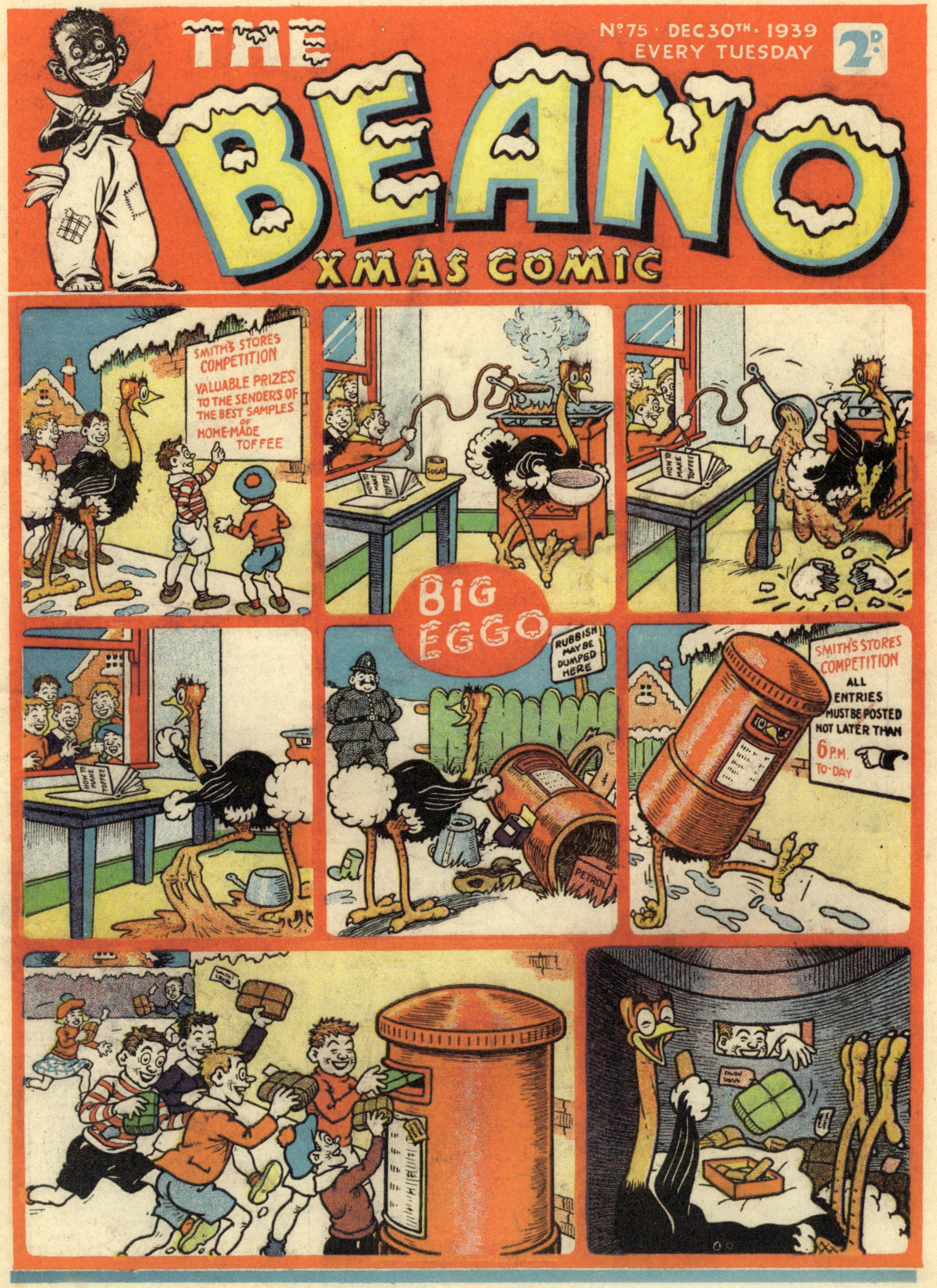

# Bumper Christmas Number

SEE KORKY SAVE THESE KIDS A ROW,
THEIR SNOWMAN'S LIKE OLD NASTY NOW.
AND THEN HE WRITES UPON THE WALL
HIS GREETINGS TO YOU ONE AND ALL.

# Christmas Holiday Number

OUR KORKY GETS THOSE TRAMPS NEW BOOTS. JUST WATCH THEM BEAM WITH JOY. THEN AFTER THAT, THEY GET OUR CAT A CHRISTMAS SPREAD, OH BOY!

## A XMAS TREAT FOR EVERY READER

# THE BEANO COMIC

No. 273—DEC. 15th, 1945  2D

## Big Eggo

"LOOK WHAT WE'VE GOT FOR XMAS!"

"HERE COMES UNCLE EGGO WE'LL GIVE HIM A SHOCK!"

"HE! HE! HE!"

"MERRY XMAS UNCLE EGGO!"

LATER

"GOSH!" "THAT WAS A DIRTY TRICK!" "WOW!"

"IT WASN'T OUR BLAME!" "WOW! STOPPIT!" "ONE GOOD TURN DESERVES ANOTHER!"

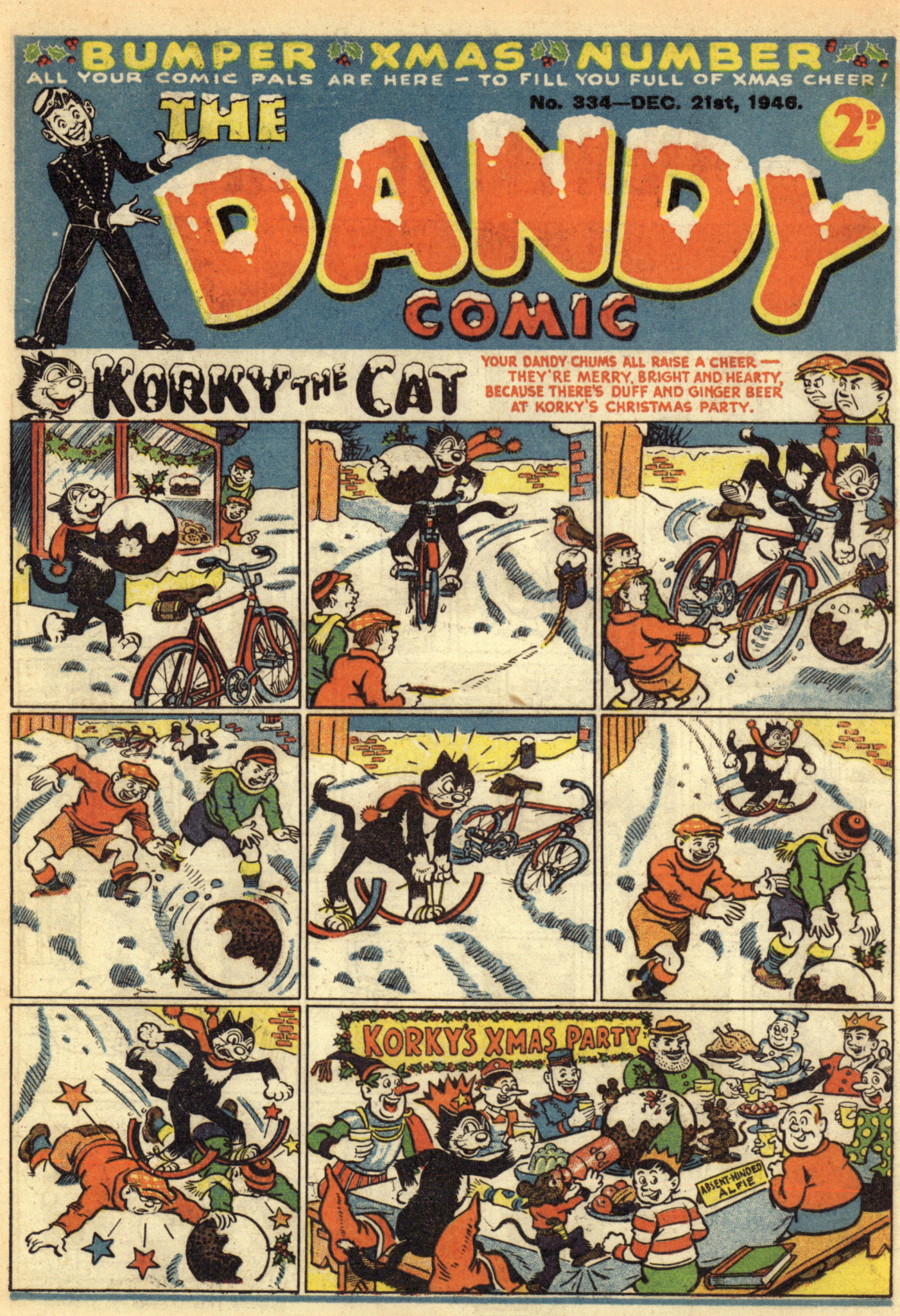

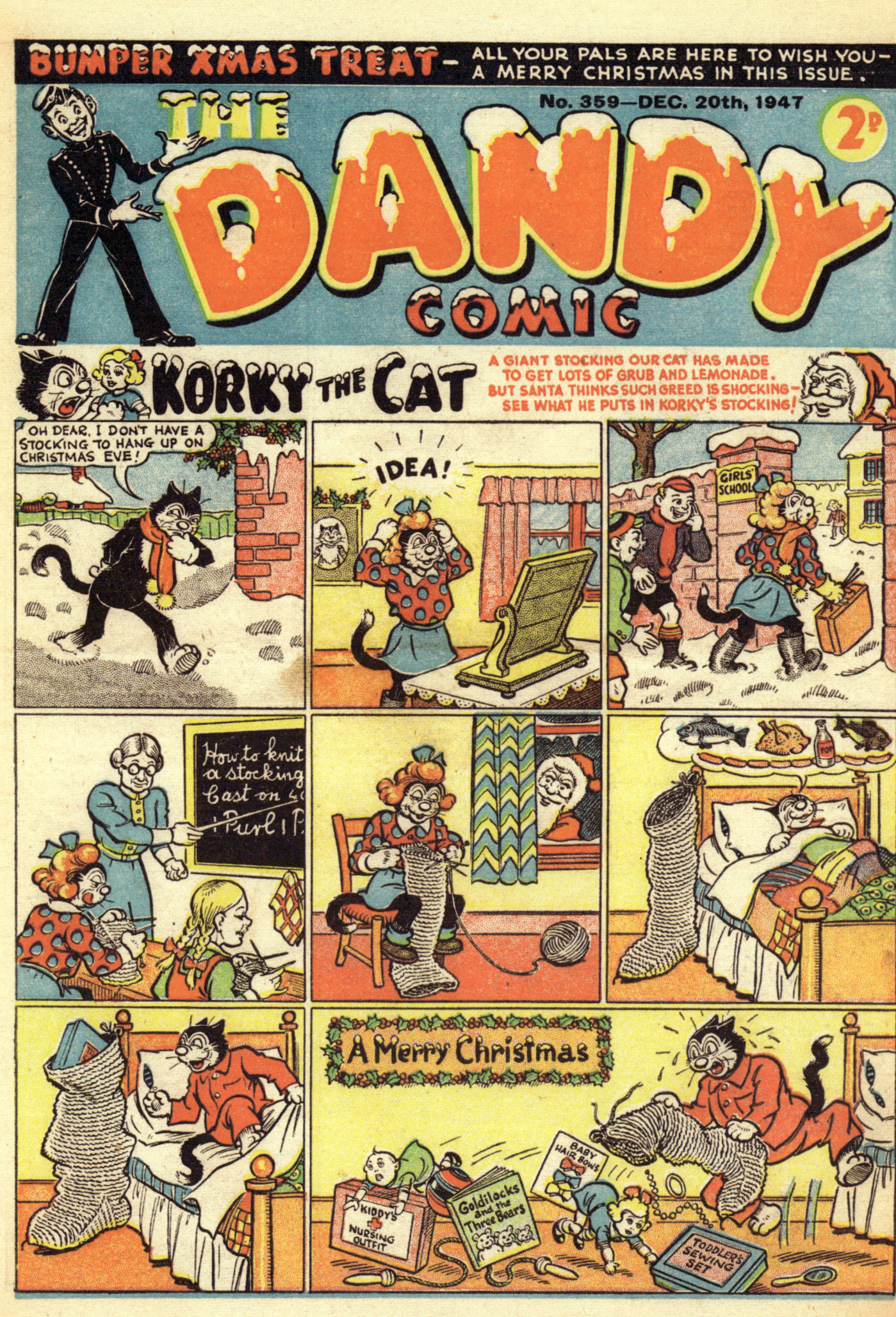

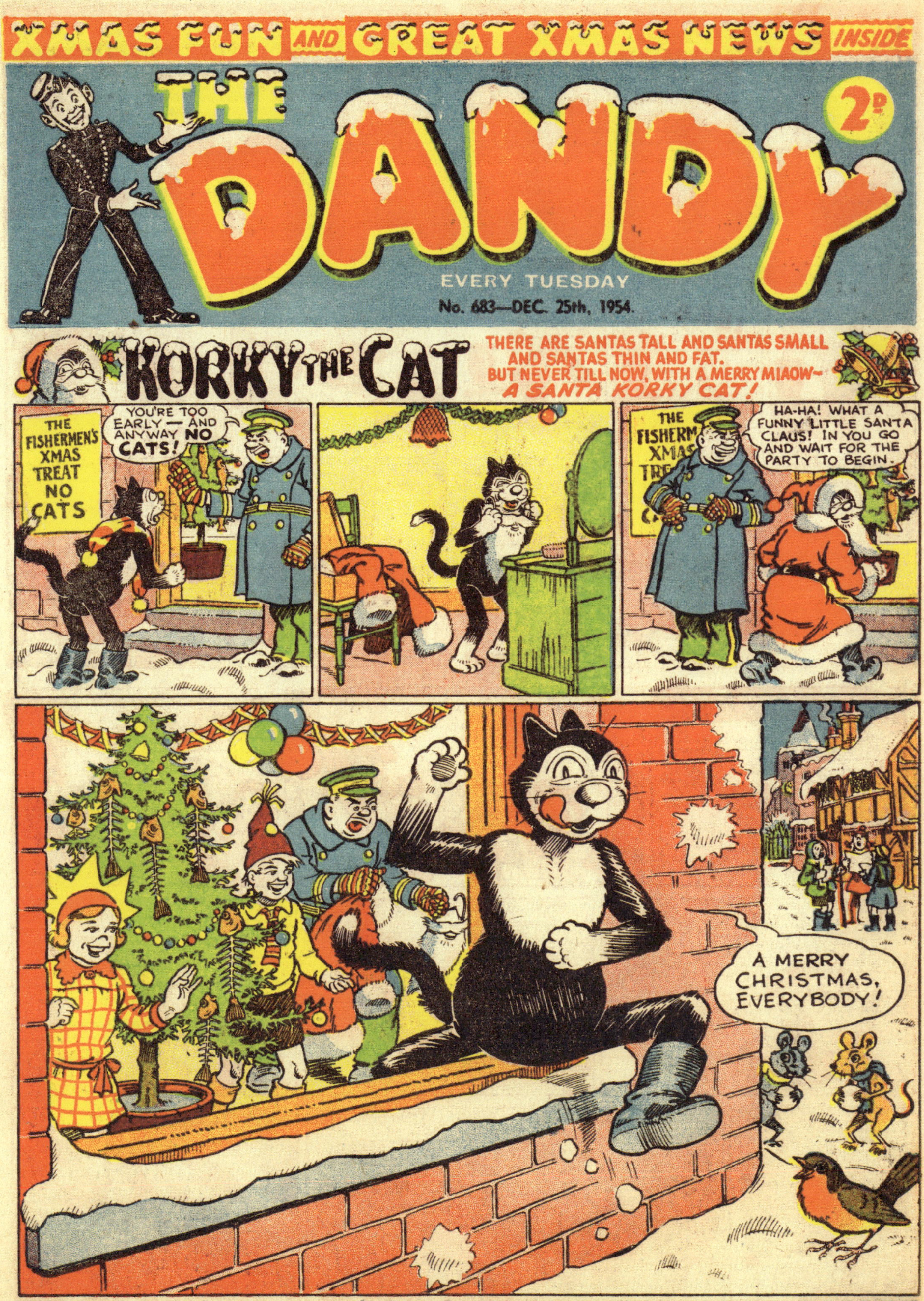

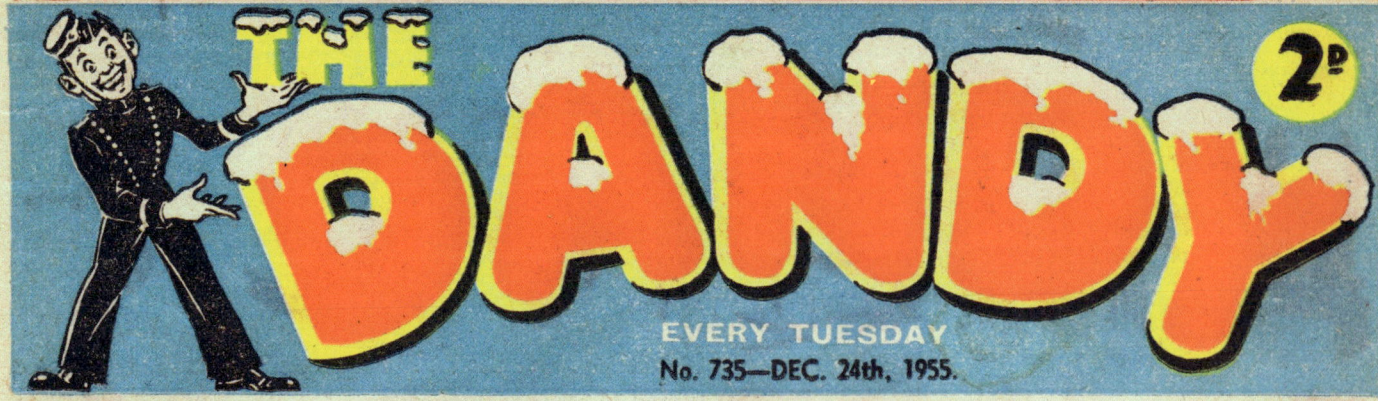

# KORKY the CAT

KORKY'S SHAKING LIKE A LEAF. HE'S SCARED STIFF, AND THE CAUSE IS HE'S JUST BEEN VISITED BY NO LESS THAN *EIGHT* DIFFERENT SANTA CLAUSES!

WELL, THAT'S MY SANTA CLAUS COSTUME READY FOR CHRISTMAS. NOW FOR SOME BISCUITS AND CHEESE.

THE MICE WON'T GET AT MY CHEESE IN THERE!

GENTLY, JOE! LOWER IT DOWN.

WE'LL GET A DOZEN GOWNS OUT OF KORKY'S BIG ONE.

I'M DREAMING! IT'S A NIGHTMARE! IT MUST HAVE BEEN THE CHEESE.

I'LL NEVER EAT CHEESE AGAIN. THE MICE CAN HAVE IT.

HAPPY CHRISTMAS TO KORKY

A MERRY CHRISTMAS TO ALL MY PALS KORKY

POOR OLD KORKY! BUT I'VE GOT A CHRISTMAS PRESENT FOR HIM!

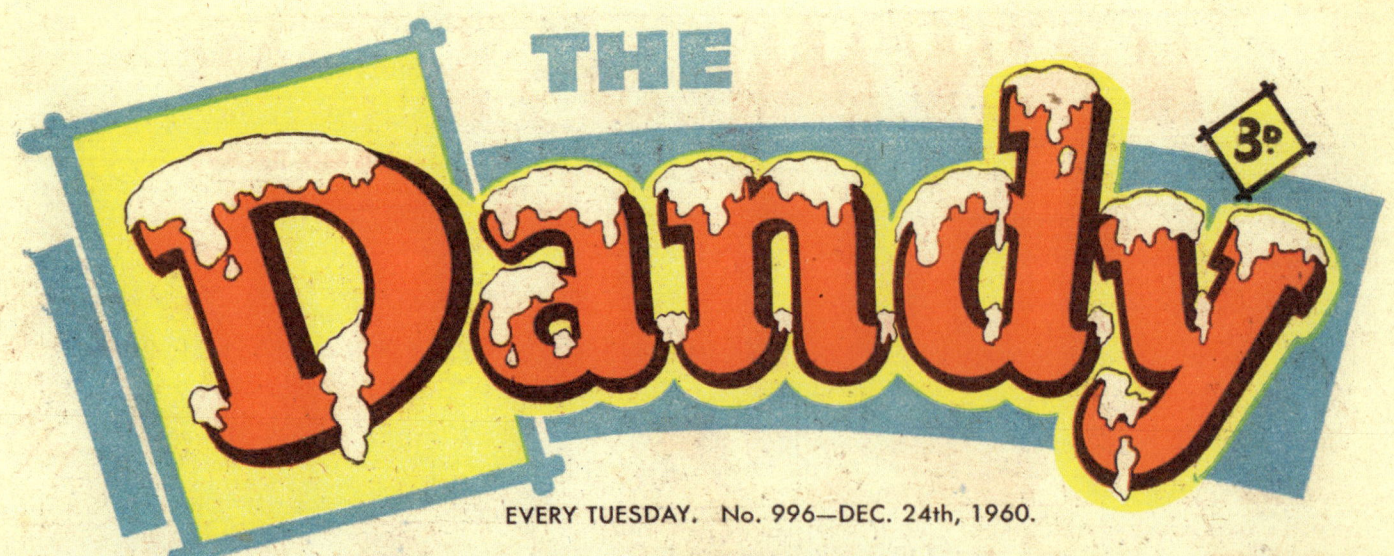

Every Tuesday. No. 1048—DECEMBER 23rd, 1961.

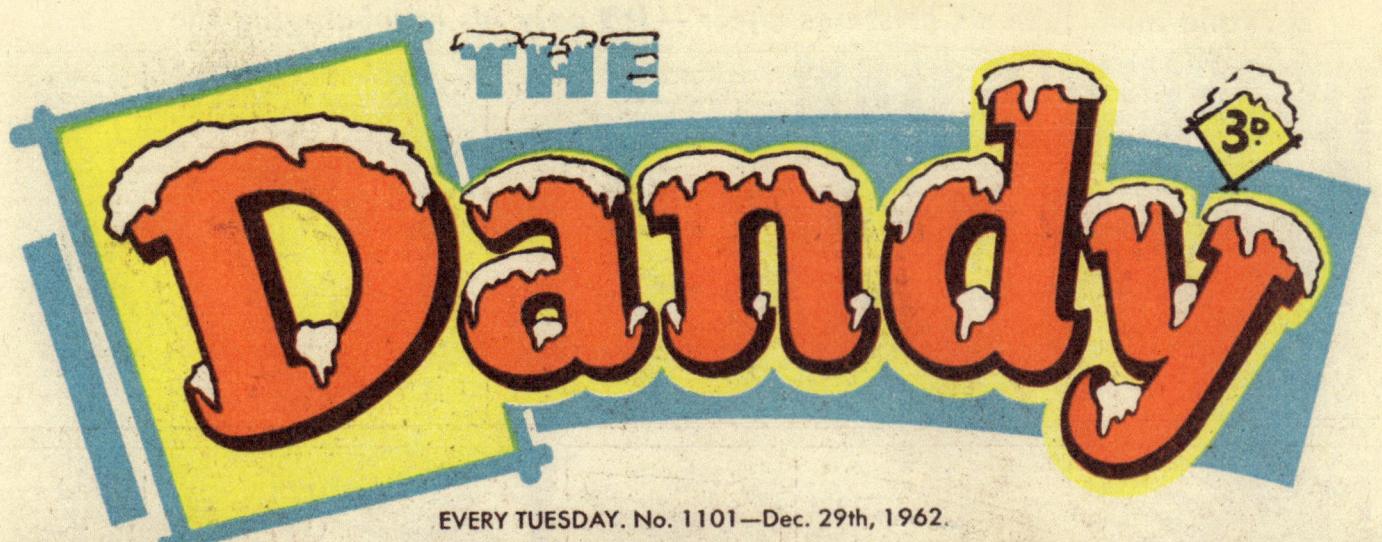

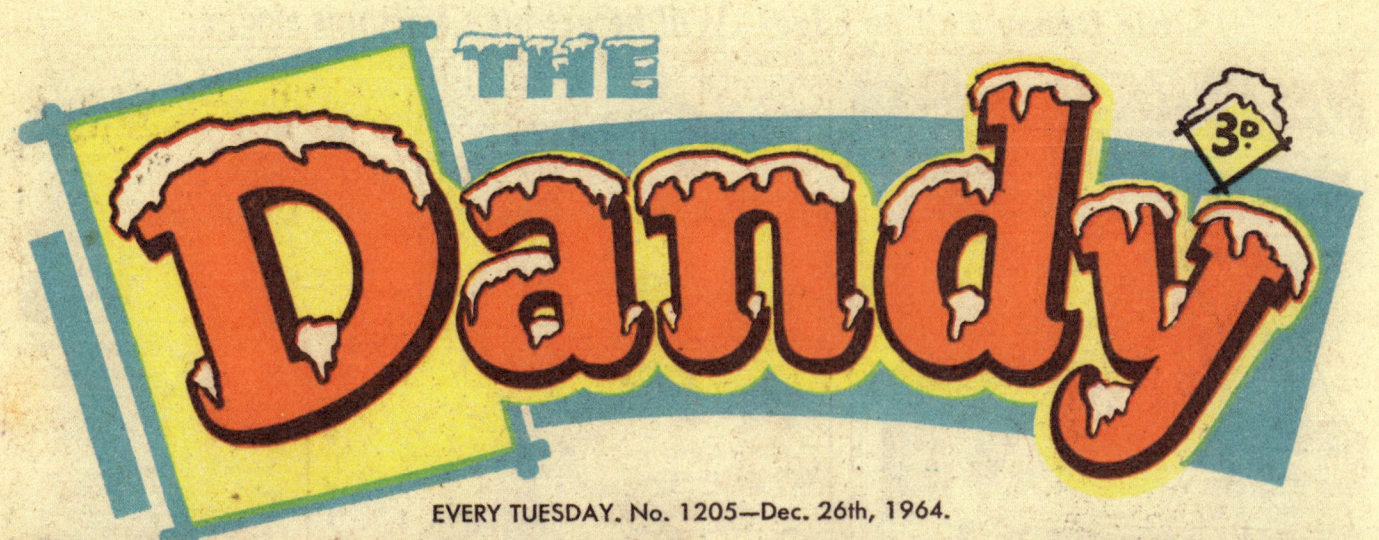

EVERY THURSDAY     No. 1171—DEC. 26th, 1964.     3D

# The Dandy

Every Tuesday. No. 1309—DEC. 24th, 1966.

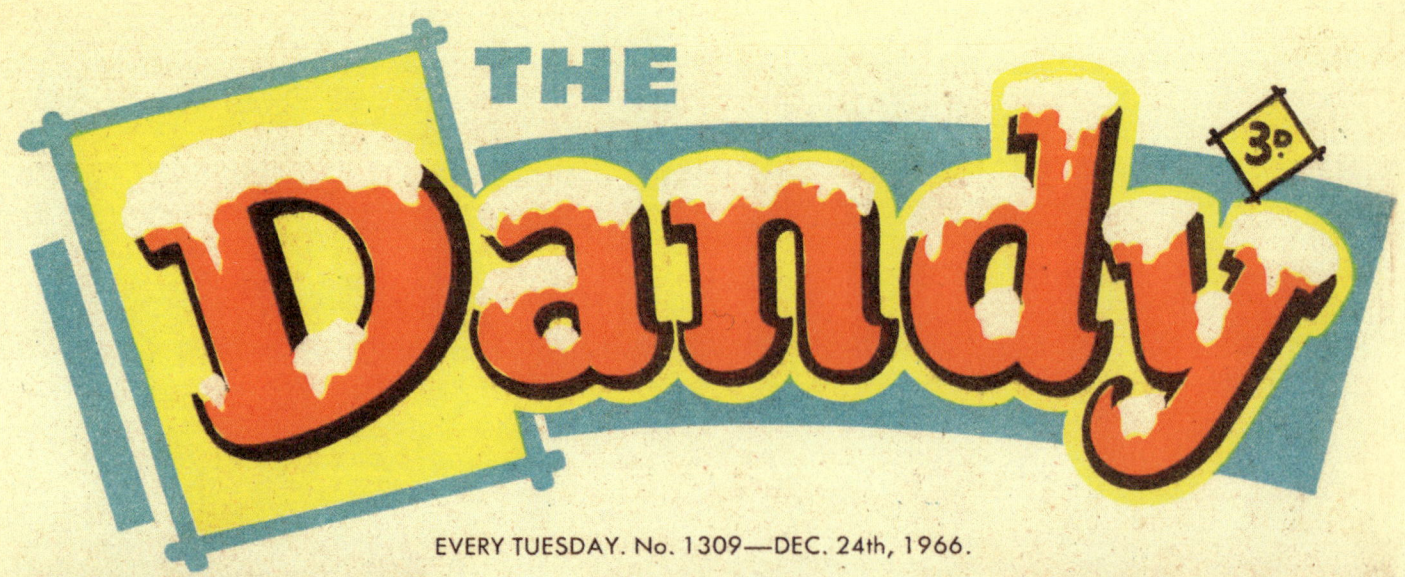